The Queens of Burlesque

Vintage Photographs of the 1940s and 1950s

Len Rothe

4880 Lower Valley Road, Atglen, PA 19310

Library of Congress Catalog Card Number: 97-80161

ISBN: 978-0-7643-0449-1
Printed in China

Book Design by Blair R.C. Loughrey

Schiffer Books are available at special discounts for bulk purchases for sales promotions or premiums. Special editions, including personalized covers, corporate imprints, and excerpts can be created in large quantities for special needs. For more information contact the publisher:

Published by Schiffer Publishing Ltd.
4880 Lower Valley Road
Atglen, PA 19310
Phone: (610) 593-1777;
Fax: (610) 593-2002
E-mail: Info@schifferbooks.com

For the largest selection of fine reference
books on this and related subjects,
please visit our web site at
www.schifferbooks.com
We are always looking for people to write books on new and related subjects.
If you have an idea for a book,
please contact us at **proposals@schifferbooks.com**

This book may be purchased
from the publisher.
Include $5.00 for shipping.
Please try your bookstore first.
You may write for a free catalog.

In Europe, Schiffer books are distributed by
Bushwood Books
6 Marksbury Ave.
Kew Gardens
Surrey TW9 4JF England
Phone: 44 (0) 20 8392-8585;
Fax: 44 (0) 20 8392-9876
E-mail: info@bushwoodbooks.co.uk
Website: www.bushwoodbooks.co.uk

Dedication

To all of the Daniels, Sarahs, Michaels, Stevens, Callies, Sydneys, and Skyes of the world, so you will know what you missed and what keeps the smile on Poppi's face and the gleam in his eye.

Introduction

To those of you who only know of burlesque through what you've heard, read, or possibly seen in a movie or on TV, you really missed a true rite-of-passage experience and a whole helluva lot of fun. To those of you who *were* there when the band struck up the introduction to the evening's featured stripteaser, you may have been sitting next to me at Minsky's and I'm willing to bet these pictures will bring back fond memories of nights that have long laid dormant and which yearn to be re-lived.

Believe me, there actually was a time in America, and not all that long ago, when entertainment was not only fun, but cheap, exciting, and on occasion, even participatory. People bought tickets (the best seats in the house costing between $5 and $7.50) to see their favorite burlesque queen perform, or perhaps to view the new tantalizer everyone couldn't wait to see. For some it was a weekly, eagerly anticipated night out, for others it was a "special occasion" event. This was one of the ways people enjoyed themselves in America before sexually explicit television and movies, sexually oriented chat pages on the Internet, almost daily sensationalized news headlines, adult book stores, topless bars, roadside sex shops and massage parlors altered the way we feel about ourselves and others, sexually.

Burlesque, however, like vaudeville (burlesque without strippers), died a quiet death in the mid-50s, for the most part unmourned. The cause of death was the "new medium" - a large 10" screen B&W television set, which brought a live picture into our home (via rabbit ears on top of the set) and cost us nothing. The first really successful shows were variety shows, actually quite similar to burlesque, with their chorus lines, comedians, musical acts, featured performers, skits, and pitchmen, one selling boxed candy (some even containing "if you're lucky, a gold wrist watch in the box"), the other selling Texaco gasoline. The primary difference between TV and burlesque was that TV left out the "girls who teased and titillated us," all of us, male and female alike: the now all but forgotten...BURLESQUE QUEENS.

And Queens they were...all had their loyal followers, wore the trappings of royalty (although sheer or pasties in many cases), and most importantly, tried their best to please the masses who fantasized about them and found pleasure in being their devoted subjects. Contrary to all you may have heard, it was good clean fun, something increasingly hard, if not impossible, to find today.

So, to those of you who wonder who the last burlesque queens were, what they looked like, the way they dressed (or undressed), this book is for you. It is real, it is fun, and strictly for your viewing pleasure and enjoyment. As you view their publicity photos, you will find that women in various states of undress are timeless; beauty and the female form hold the same intrigue and fascination for us today as they did in the past. Some things never change...thank God.

However, if you want to get the most enjoyment out of this book, try to imagine all the sights and sounds of an actual burlesque show: these torrid beauties bumping and grinding (almost in time to the loud brassy music) as they really appear to be "taking it off" (to the lusty shouts of the anxious audience); the chorus line (a bevy of "beauties" comprising "somebody important's friend"), either too thin or too heavy, but still with dreams of "developing" into a burlesque queen, in a time before silicone or liposuction; the somewhat inappropriate whispered remark among buddies out for the night; the wife or girlfriend trying to pretend she's not really enjoying the show despite her laughter and squeals of feigned shock (and maybe even a tinge of envy); the occasional heavy breather in a trench coat (sitting way in the back); the smoke filled theatre (despite warnings to the contrary); the frivolity, camaraderie and laughter. But most of all, think of all the fun and memories ...if only YOU were there.

Direct From Hollywood,
Za-Za Amour
"The Bouncing Parisan"
(1956)

Ann "Bang Bang" Arbor

"The Million Dollar Figure"

More of the Fabulous...

Ann "Bang Bang" Arbor

Gene Laverne
Buffalo, N.Y.

Yes! This is the Famous...

Nejla Ates

"The Exquisite Turkish Delight"

"The Girl You've Heard So Much About."

The Appropriately Attired...

Bonnie Bell

Bonnie Boya

From Elegant to Electrifying...

Sherry Britton

Bobbie Bruce

"The Barroness Bon Bon"

Garbo
CHICAGO

Leaving Her Trail of Fire...

The Comet

Lorraine Cooper

Thr Lovely and Exciting...

Dagmar

Bloom

Yvette Dare

"Exotic danseuse, whose unique specialty, "The Dance of the Sacred Parrott", is acclaimed by critics as one of the most thrilling and artistic performances ever seen...."

Bubbles Darlene

"America's Most Exciting Body"

Dirian Dennis

Princess Do May
"The Cherokee Half-Breed"
(1956)

Lotus DuBois

"The Parisian Un-Cover Girl"

Maurice Seymour

Marcia Eddington

Garbo
CHICAGO

Sen Lee Fu

"The Most Exotic Dancer of Them All"

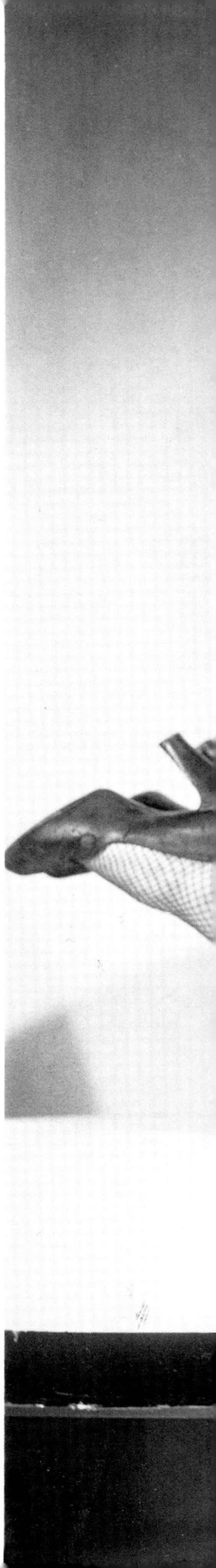

Garbo
CHICA

Blaze Fury

"The Human Heatwave"

"Often Imitated, Never Equalled"

Gene Laverne of
Buffalo, N.Y.

Helena Gardner

"The Bewitching Beauty"

Garbo
CHICAGO

Bruno of Hollywood Nyc

Winnie Garrett

"The Flaming Redhead"

Fresh New and Exciting Personality Direct From Hollywood...

Gilda

"Hollywood's Golden Goddess"

(1955)

Rita Grable

"Gorgeous Blonde Stocking Model"

James J.
Kriegsmann
N.Y.

"The Girl Who Has Everything"

Betty Howard

"The Girl With The Big Beautiful Blue Eyes"

Bruno of Hollywood

Pat
"Amber"
Halladay

Garbo
CHICAGO

Garbo

The photo says it all.

Kay Hanna

"America's Most Gorgeous Blonde"

Jill Huntley

"Miss Dean of Tease"

Jame
Kriegsma

Irene

"Towering Blonde Beauty"

James J. Kriegsmann N.Y.

The graceful and Elegant...

J'Aimee

BRUNO
of
Hollywood
Nyc

Mickey Jones

rbo
CHICAGO

Lili LaMont

"The Academy Award Winner"

(1956)

Tana
Louise
"The Heat Wave"

Murray
Korman
N.Y.

Lorelei

"The Girl in the Oyster Shell"

Maurice Seymour
Chicago

The Lovely and Charismatic...

Helen Lovett

Murray
Korman
N.Y.

James J.
Kriegsmann
N.Y.

Jan Mavis

"The Sunshine Girl"

Scarlett O'Hara

"The Exciting Lassie with the Classy Chassis"

(1954)

Newark's Favorite Persona...

Penny Page

"The S-E-X Girl"

RUNO
of
Hollywood
NYC

Valerie Parks

"Your Favorite Blonde Striptease"

Bruno
of
Hollywood
Nyc

Ann Perri

"The Parisian Jane Russell"

(1955)

Garbo
CHICAGO

"Miss T-N-T Herself"

Pepper Powell

"Torrid Titian Haired Tantalizer"

More of the Sensuous...

Pepper Powell

"Hottest Thing Since the Chicago Fire"

James
Kriegsmann

Jean Richey

"Queen Of The Rollers"

John E. Reed
HOLLYWOOD

The Seductive and Beautiful...

Countess Ruhkova

Sequin

"Beauty to the 4th Dimension"

Continental Blonde Beauty...

Siri

"Dutch Doll"

Sonia

"The Sultry Sophisticate"

Gene Laverne of
Buffalo, N.Y.

Crystal Starr

"More Bounce to the Ounce"

"I make $500 a week. I own my own house in Gardenia, California, and I have a car - all paid for. My parents have a house around the corner from mine. I've got all that and I'm just twenty one. I think I'm doing all right." -Crystal Starr, 1955

Direct from Massachusetts...

Lisa Starr

PAUL WINIK
OF
BOSTON

The Absolutely Beautiful...

Lili St Cyr

Bernard
Hollywood

Encore, Encore...

Lili St Cyr

ohn E. Reed
•HOLLYWOOD•

Hold on to Your Hats...

Tempest Storm

Robin Sweet

"The Newest Body in Burlesque"

The Intoxicating...

Tequila

Val de Val

Maurice Seymour
Chicago

Vallkyra

"Toast of the Coast"

Romaine

The Sultry and Seductive...

Trudy Wayne

(1954)

Garbo
CHICAGO

Direct From Los Angeles...

Evelyn West

The Fabulous...

Zorita